Comments on other *Amazing Stories* from readers & reviewers

*"Tightly written volumes filled with lots of wit and humour
about famous and infamous Canadians."*
Eric Shackleton, *The Globe and Mail*

*"The heightened sense of drama and intrigue, combined with a
good dose of human interest is what sets* Amazing Stories *apart."*
Pamela Klaffke, *Calgary Herald*

*"This is popular history as it should be... For this price,
buy two and give one to a friend."*
Terry Cook, a reader from Ottawa, on **Rebel Women**

*"Glasner creates the moment of the explosion itself in
graphic detail...she builds detail upon gruesome detail
to create a convincingly authentic picture."*
Peggy McKinnon, *The Sunday Herald*, on **The Halifax Explosion**

*"It was wonderful...I found I could not put it down.
I was sorry when it was completed."*
Dorothy F. from Manitoba on **Marie-Anne Lagimodière**

*"Stories are rich in description, and bristle
with a clever, stylish realness."*
Mark Weber, *Central Alberta Advisor*, on **Ghost Town Stories II**

*"A compelling read. Bertin...has selected only the most intriguing
tales, which she narrates with a wealth of detail."*
Joyce Glasner, *New Brunswick Reader*, on **Strange Events**

*"The resulting book is one readers will want to share
with all the women in their lives."*
Lynn Martel, *Rocky Mountain Outlook*, on **Women Explorers**

THE LIFE OF
A LOYALIST

THE LIFE OF A LOYALIST

A Tale of Survival in Old Nova Scotia

HISTORY

by Cathleen Fillmore

PUBLISHED BY ALTITUDE PUBLISHING CANADA LTD.
1500 Railway Avenue, Canmore, Alberta T1W 1P6
www.altitudepublishing.com
1-800-957-6888

Publisher	Stephen Hutchings
Associate Publisher	Kara Turner
Series Editor	Jill Foran
Maps	Scott Manktelow

We acknowledge the financial support of the Government
of Canada through the Book Publishing Industry Development
Program (BPIDP) for our publishing activities.

Altitude GreenTree Program
Altitude Publishing will plant twice as many trees as were used
in the manufacturing of this product.

National Library of Canada Cataloguing in Publication Data

Fillmore, Cathleen
    The life of a loyalist / Cathleen Fillmore.

(Amazing stories)
Includes bibliographical references.
ISBN 1-55153-944-6

1. Davis, Christina, 1765-1858. 2. United Empire loyalists--Nova Scotia--
Brier Island. 3. Frontier and pioneer life--Nova Scotia--Brier Island.
4. United Empire loyalists--Nova Scotia--Brier Island--Biography.
5. Brier Island (N.S.)--Biography. I. Title. II. Series: Amazing stories
(Canmore, Alta.)

FC2345.B74Z49 2004   971.6'3202'092   C2003-906768-8

An application for the trademark for Amazing Stories[TM]
has been made and the registered trademark is pending.

Printed and bound in Canada by Friesens
2 4 6 8 9 7 5 3 1

Cover: An idealized image of Loyalists landing
on a rocky Nova Scotian coast.

Lovingly dedicated to my three remarkable nieces:
Eileen Rogers, Diane Rogers, and Christine Fillmore.

Author's Note

Since records in the 18th and early 19th century are unreliable, many of the facts in this book cannot be verified. Some are based on conjecture and oral histories, passed from one generation to the next. This book is an attempt to capture the history of a remarkable woman's life as accurately as possible, given the scanty records.

Cathleen Fillmore

Contents

Prologue

December 10, 1816

My dear cousin,

I fear I have only bad news to impart and have hesitated long before sending this letter, not wanting to worry you.

How I miss your shining countenance! And how I wish we were closer in geography, though knowing we will ever be near in heart gives me some comfort in these dark uncertain times.

You will remember the fateful letter I wrote a few months ago telling you of our financial difficulties this past summer. On June 6th, the sky blackened and we were visited with extreme weather conditions — several inches of snow and some hail. It ruined the crops my sons had already planted and although we quickly housed the sheep, already shorn, in the barn, each and every one died of the cold. The crops rotted in the field. 'Twas a black day when, having no sustenance for my cow, I had to send her to slaughter. Those dreadful months were truly insupportable and some others have left the Island, seeking a more hospitable climate.

The Life of a Loyalist

Forgive me for dwelling on past events, it is simply that I thought I had been given the worst life could give me — surely in the past few years, I have suffered as much as any human could bear. Yet a worse fate may well lie ahead.

Still reeling from the 'summer that never was' and our reduced financial circumstances, I received just a month later an official letter from a local lawyer stating that our neighbour had laid claim to our land. Yes, the same neighbour we have been disputing with for years who has been all too eager to claim our well-tilled land and herb gardens for himself. Never mind that my ministrations saved his baby from the croup one dark winter night. After much negotiation among ourselves with local officials, the Hatches are now threatening to take it to court.

Martha, dear, I feel sure you will forgive me, now that you know the circumstances, for not having written sooner. Please write a letter in your inimitable fashion, dispensing consolation and advice. I fear I must rescind the invitation I extended you to come and visit us although your company would be good tonic indeed. I may not even have a roof, however humble, over my head to offer you. All this strife and struggle to only end up just where I began, in New York, when our home was taken from us.

Prologue

It's a black star that is above me, my dear.

With deep affection,

I remain,
Your loving cousin, Margaret

Chapter 1
Born Amid a
Brewing Revolution

Born December 21, 1765, to Catherine and Adam Hubbard, Christiana Margaret Hubbard was simply called Margaret. Her parents were German immigrants who had settled in New York, where her father worked as a shoemaker. While little is known about Margaret's upbringing, it can be said with some certainty that she was taught values and skills that served her well during a lifetime that was, by any standards, remarkable.

The first few years of Margaret's life in upper New York State were peaceful and uneventful. But as she grew, so did the tensions between England and the 13 American colonies — to the point where a rupture was inevitable. As a result, Margaret's life, and the lives of countless others, was to take an unexpected turn.

By 1774, when Margaret was only 10 years old, conflict between England and the American colonies had reached fever pitch. While some colonists — the Loyalists — felt that the dispute was the result of greedy merchants unwilling to pay their fair taxes to England, others — the Rebels — were armed and ready to go to battle to fight to the death for their independence. Loyalists countered that there was nothing to gain in independence, that one form of oppression would simply be traded for another: "Which is better — to be ruled by one tyrant 3000 miles away or 3000 tyrants not one mile away?" was the question they asked each other. And the answer was simple — better the enemy they knew.

But it was a dangerous time to be loyal to the Crown. The divisive war had pitted neighbour against neighbour and father against son. Often one family member publicly accused another of Loyalist sympathies. Those who defied the more popular revolutionary sentiments were shunned and punished. Men were beaten and imprisoned, farms were confiscated and sometimes burned, and women and children were separated from their families and sent into exile. Everyone, even the clergy, took sides. Preacher John Lathrop spoke of the conflict from the pulpit in December 1774, lamenting "the present distracted state of our public affairs. Look to our port and you'll see it blocked up with British ships of war ... Our public streets, our most pleasant walks, are filled with armed soldiers. All things wear the shocking appearance of war. Between Great Britain and the colonies, between fellow subjects, between brethren!"

Men suspected of being Tories (Loyalists) were tarred and feathered — a vicious practice designed to humiliate the victim and set fear in the hearts of onlookers. It did far more than that — the tar was scalding hot and left deep scars that became a lifetime reminder of a brutal period in history.

The Loyalist Cause

Margaret's father, Adam Hubbard, took England's side in the conflict that was to become the American Revolution and joined the British army in 1777. After just two months, he was taken prisoner by the revolutionaries and spent seven months in jail in Albany before he was transferred to Pennsylvania, far from his family. As Adam was languishing in jail, the British were busy evacuating Loyalists from the city of Philadelphia. Adam was out of their reach and their protection. Word of the evacuation and possible retaliation spread through the prison, bringing little comfort and much added concern to the inmates.

With Adam in prison, Margaret's mother, Catherine, struggled to keep the farm going and the family fed. Thirteen-year-old Margaret took on adult responsibilities as she helped her mother with the younger children. It was Margaret who kept the children out of harm's way the memorable day that Catherine tried unsuccessfully to negotiate with the Rebels who arrived to confiscate the 80-hectare family farm.

Catherine knew any protest would be in vain and that the family was lucky to escape with their lives. The land the Hubbards had worked so hard to clear, the home they'd built with their own hands, was gone. The family was left with nothing and had to depend on the kindness of relatives and neighbours. Knowing they were a burden to others was the worst blow yet for these self-sufficient and proud people.

Eventually, Adam managed to escape from prison and make his way back home. Through the rumour mill he got word that his farm had been taken and sold. His overriding concern, though, was whether or not he'd find his family — and in what condition he would find them.

Though he was almost unrecognizable, Margaret knew immediately that the emaciated man she saw walking down the road was her dear father and she ran to greet him. Her mother was close behind her. It was a wonderful reunion. Though they had few material possessions, they still had each other. And they made plans, if worse came to worst, to leave the country and find shelter in Canada. In spite of all evidence to the contrary, though, the family continued to hope that Britain would retain control of the American colonies, the Rebels would come to their senses, and peace would be restored.

Adam Hubbard was determined to do his part to keep America loyal. Once he recovered from his ordeal he promptly re-enlisted in the British army, where he stayed for another three years. Perhaps because of the chaos of the times, he was never paid for these three years of service. The family was utterly destitute, yet they clung to their dimming hope that the Loyalist cause would prevail. (Many years later, when widowed, Catherine made a successful bid for compensation for the three years her husband served as a soldier in the army without pay.)

Adam was still in the army when word came in 1781 that Lord Cornwallis had surrendered to the Rebels in Virginia. It was becoming distressingly clear that the war was ending and that the Rebels were the victors. This was a bitter pill for those colonists who had remained loyal to England and who had fervently hoped that Britain would somehow regain control. It was especially bitter for Adam, who had not only been imprisoned for his beliefs, but who had lost his farm and his livelihood to boot.

In peaceful times, Margaret would have been married and starting her own family by the age of 17. Now her future was uncertain and it seemed she would be leaving for Canada with her family before long. Though she had her eye on a former lawyer, Eathel Davis, Margaret knew she was needed at home and marriage, for the moment, was out of the question. In the meantime, the two stole precious moments here and there to see each other and romance blossomed despite the tumultuous times.

Eathel Davis, whose parents were of Welsh descent, came from Derby, Connecticut, a fishing and shipbuilding town with a population of 1000. Early on in the conflict,

Eathel abandoned his law practice and joined the army that was loyal to the King. It's not clear whether he joined the British army of his own accord or if he was carried off against his will — a common practice in those days. Whatever his motivation, he must have been persuaded he was on the right side because, like his future father-in-law, Eathel stayed and fought with the Loyalist troops until 1783.

Betrayed

Hopes were cautiously high among the Loyalists that Sir Guy Carleton, former governor of Canada and now appointed the commander-in-chief of His Majesty's Forces in America, would set things right when he set foot on American soil in 1782. The Loyalists firmly believed that Carleton came "to gratify his Majesty's Expectations and the ardent wishes of his People for Peace on equal and honourable Terms." Peace, to those loyal to the Crown, meant reconciliation with England along with certain reforms.

However, it soon became clear that Carleton had come not to reunite the colonies with England, but to acknowledge the independence of the 13 states. The Loyalists were stunned and felt completely betrayed by this pronouncement. They had risked their lives, their homes, and their families to defend the King, and now the King no longer supported the cause they'd been willing to die for. They'd been abandoned and were left with no other option but to leave America for their own protection.

Defeated, the Loyalists insisted on one condition concerning their relocation. They told Carleton they wanted homes in a land that still belonged to the British. Obligingly, Carleton looked to Nova Scotia — a province that had already been advertising in the colonies for new settlers, and one known for its neutral position on the war.

The Lure of Nova Scotia

Nova Scotians had been following the battle between the American colonies and Britain, and many had considered whether they too would join the revolution. However, being a new colony, and very dependent on Britain for trade, they decided against joining the fight for independence. "We were almost all of us born in North England," protested Yarmouth residents. "We have fathers, brothers, and sisters in that country." Nova Scotians would have made a poor militia, in any case, scattered as they were in small coastal communities.

While most did not want to join in the fight for independence, they did not want to join the British army fighting against the Rebels, either. They aimed for neutrality. If they took up arms, it would be purely in self-defence — against conscription. "The Canadian peasantry," sighed Carleton, "not only deserted their duty but numbers of them have taken up arms against the Crown." With little opposition, by the end of the war, both Quebec and Nova Scotia were firmly under British control. As insurance against possible insurgence, New Brunswick, populated with people loyal to

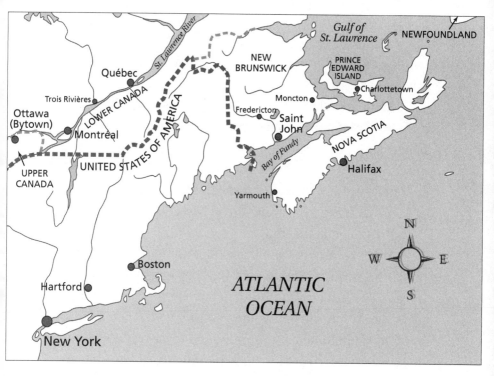

Nova Scotia's earliest transportation route was the sea,
with regular trade routes to New York and beyond

England, was created as a buffer province between Nova
Scotia and America.

The new British government turned to Massachusetts,
Connecticut, and Rhode Island — colonies that were experi-
encing land scarcity and soil exhaustion — and offered the
inhabitants generous land grants in the territory of Nova

Scotia. While Nova Scotia gained roughly 8000 settlers from this campaign, there was still plenty of land that needed tending and tilling, and the territory welcomed the Loyalist refugees with open arms.

Another pull towards Nova Scotia came from those who had already left the colonies and settled in this sparsely populated land. They knew full well that their generous land grant would be worthless in an isolated place, so they encouraged their friends and relatives to join them, quite possibly painting a rosier picture of Nova Scotia than conditions warranted at the time.

Some recruiters were paid a bounty for each "tourist" they brought in, so they would travel to England, Scotland, Ireland, or Germany and bring in anyone they could round up by describing the new land in exaggerated, fanciful terms as a land of unlimited opportunity. And these recruiters were not choosy. Their catch included criminals, along with the sick, the old, and the poor.

Two large evacuations from the American colonies had already set sail for Nova Scotia by the time the Hubbards decided to leave. One of the earliest departures took place on St. Patrick's Day in 1776, when 11,000 British troops, 1000 Loyalists, and 78 ships left Boston.

Before the war was over, more than 100,000 Loyalists fled the 13 American colonies. Not all were destined for Canada. Some went to England and others to the West Indies. Trying to safely transport such an enormous number of people was a logistical nightmare for the British. They attempted to provide at least one good suit and two pairs of stockings and shoes for each man, a blanket for each person, food for the journey, plus an axe and a hatchet to begin constructing life anew in Canada. While the British did their utmost to provide properly for the Loyalists, their ability to supply the necessities of life for these refugees was stretched to the limit. A British report published in 1790 stated that relocation of the Loyalists cost the British $15.5 million dollars. Even so, the pumping in of funds couldn't prevent many people from dying either during the journey or in their first encounter with a cold Canadian winter.

Last to Leave
Resisting the inevitability of the war's outcome, the Hubbard family hung in till the bitter end. They were part of the last wave of refugee evacuations. While their tenacity would serve them well in later years, the hard truth was that their only choice was to leave the land they loved and to start over in a new and unknown country. For the two young lovers, Margaret Hubbard and Eathel Davis, the thought of being separated was unthinkable. So, in anticipation of leaving for Canada, they married in a simple ceremony in July 1783.

The wedding ceremony was held in the Lutheran Church of New York, where Margaret had been christened. (In a sign of the times, Rebels had burned the local Lutheran church.) There was only a muted family celebration. At this

The British fleet, carrying thousands of Loyalists,
ready to leave New York

point in history, there were many more funerals than weddings taking place. Not only was it difficult to feel lighthearted, but without funds the family couldn't afford to supply food and drink to friends and neighbours, though a few dropped by to offer congratulations. As Loyalists, neither Margaret nor Eathel's family wanted to draw any attention to themselves. With the loss of most of their possessions and their farm, they had already paid a high price for their British allegiance. But at least they could be thankful that their families had not been torn apart, as others had, by political differences, and thus far neither family had lost a member to war.

Eathel was happy to flee the pandemonium in America and make a fresh start in a new country with his young bride. His future children, he hoped, would live peaceful and productive lives. United, but without further recourse, Adam Hubbard, his wife Catherine, and their five surviving children, including Margaret and her husband, Eathel, boarded the war frigate, the *Clinton*, in late October 1783.

The family had gathered what belongings they could carry with them, along with a few paltry provisions. Precious family heirlooms from Germany had already been lost when the Rebels had confiscated the Hubbard farm, but a few cherished possessions remained hidden among clothing. It was painful to pick and choose the most essential and useful belongings to take on the trip. One was a leather-bound book that was very dear to Margaret. Printed in Germany in 1760, it contained the teachings of a religious leader named Hartmann. Another was a pair of brass candleholders, handcrafted in Germany.

The Hubbard and Davis families paid a price for holding firm to their belief that America and England would reconcile under the British flag. By the time they chose to emigrate from the American colonies, the prime parcels of land in Nova Scotia had already been granted. The Hubbards were given land that was considered the bottom of the heap — in Quebec, which then included Ontario.

The chill of winter was already in the air as the *Clinton* pulled out from the harbour headed for Quebec — a chill that would get increasingly bitter as the ship moved out to sea. The *Clinton* was large enough to house hundreds of refugees and dozens of crewmembers easily, if not comfortably. There was a surgeon on duty who operated out of a sick room on the lower deck.

The galley, where all meals were cooked, was inspected regularly by crewmembers since the coal stove represented a major fire hazard. The ship's food provisions were stored at the bottom of the ship, which held wooden barrels of water and beer along with salted beef, pork, butter, peas, raisins, suet, oatmeal, and marmalade to stave off scurvy. A separate room held tons of biscuits and flour.

As they sailed into the unknown, Margaret and her younger sister, Ana Maria, stood on deck with dozens of other refugees, their blankets wrapped tightly around them, and watched their homeland fade into the fog. While they had a sense of sadness, at least they finally felt safe under the auspices of the British army.

After several days on the open sea, however, any optimism the refugees had about building a new future was displaced by despair and desperation, which increased every day they were aboard the *Clinton*. Not only were the waves treacherous, but the weather also turned bitterly cold. For Margaret, the greatest challenge was to keep her brothers and sisters wrapped in dry, warm clothing, and to make sure they had enough to eat.

The journey was a rough one, lasting four excruciatingly

long weeks. Margaret's parents, already in a weakened condition, fared terribly during the voyage. The elder Hubbards, being too weak to go up on deck, suffered from severe seasickness. As Margaret watched and worried over her parents, she vowed to learn what she could about healing. Her mother had taught her all she'd learned about healing in Germany, and had assured Margaret, when she had to drop out of school at an early age, that she had an aptitude for healing that couldn't be obtained by "book-learning." In the meantime, Margaret did what she could. The two major difficulties during the long journey were keeping clean with very limited washing facilities and keeping the family's spirits up in the face of such adversity. Low spirits soon led to illness, Margaret noted. At night, they said prayers, sang hymns in German, and talked about the future in a new land — all of which helped lift their spirits.

Battered by storms and high winds, it was a solid month before a particularly severe storm forced the ship to take refuge in Shelburne, Nova Scotia. Towards the end of the trip, food supplies were perilously low onboard. It was early November and the refugees were feeling the effects of exposure to cold and hunger — they'd long since given up caring where they landed just as long as they did.

Dizzy from being at sea such a long time, the Hubbards and Davises set foot on shore, not knowing whether they'd stay in Shelburne for the winter or continue on to Quebec. It soon became clear that Catherine and Adam were in no shape to travel, and Margaret was unwilling to leave her parents, so the two families decided to spend the winter in Shelburne. Once again, a seemingly inconsequential decision dictated by external circumstances was to alter the family's destiny.

Chapter 2
Portrait of the Times

he *Clinton* anchored as close to the shore as possible and then transported the weary passengers to land in smaller boats. The process took a long time, but since her parents were so unwell, Margaret's family was one of the first to leave the ship and set foot on shore. They soon discovered that thousands of other Loyalists had arrived at Shelburne before them, turning this once small port village into a bustling city almost overnight.

James Courtney, one of the first Loyalists to inhabit Shelburne, recorded his initial impressions of the place: "On our arrival here dark woods and dismal Rocks Cover'd the ground (which belonged to the Associated Loyalists). On my first going on shore after traveling five or six hours, returned quite dismayed, and yet in the Course of my Ramble knocked down two brace of Partridges and one Hare, next time went further [and] still returned dissatisfied, I tho't Hunger look'd every wretch in the face that could not hunt or shoot for his subsistence ...

"We have got our town Lotts which is just large for a good House and Small garden ... Since the Trees are cut/good down the Ground looks ... far preferable to any about Halifax ... [I am now] determined to stay and think to do exceeding well."

The influx of more than 10,000 Loyalists in a very short period had turned Shelburne into the fourth-largest city in North America. It was a city that was suffering from the pains of rapid growth while at the same time benefiting from the expertise and hard labour of its new inhabitants.

The Hubbard and Davis families had the advantage of landing in a city that not only promised freedom of religion and responsible government, but also offered established commercial enterprises such as fishing, shipbuilding, agriculture, commerce, lumbering, and trading. Roads, bridges, and ferries were under construction, there were schools for the children, and newspapers had been published there for over 30 years. In other words, Shelburne was a reasonably civilized city.

The Hubbards decided to stay put for the winter and travel to Quebec in the spring. They inquired into the possibility of getting a land grant in Shelburne but, although Adam Hubbard and Eathel Davis were both highly revered for their services to the Crown, the land-grant system in the city was now in tatters and the best land had already been claimed and settled, legitimately or otherwise, by those who had arrived earlier. There was not even temporary lodging space available.

With heavy hearts, the Hubbards, along with Margaret, returned to the boat to stay until accommodations were found. There they were joined by other Loyalists who had been unable to find land for themselves. The homeless Loyalists picked up daily food rations from hastily constructed street kitchens. Meanwhile, Eathel remained in town, talking to people and looking for a place for his family to live. He discovered that some residents of Shelburne welcomed the new influx of fellow Loyalists, while others resented the arrival of yet more people and more demands on tools and food supplies.

Eathel soon encountered former neighbours from his hometown who had arrived in Shelburne a few months earlier. They invited him and his extended family to share their newly constructed house on the outskirts of the city. Eathel helped to build an addition that would comfortably house the Hubbards, and it was there that they spent the bitterly cold winter.

Settling Shelburne

Shelburne, formerly called Port Razir, anglicized to Port Roseway in 1720, existed long before any Loyalist set foot on shore — it had already been inhabited for hundreds of years. Champlain bypassed the port in 1604 because the rocky shoals looked too treacherous to navigate. Braver souls who made their way safely into the harbour became the first European settlers, sharing the land with the original inhabitants, the Algonquin First Nation. The settlers were rewarded with abundant fish, as much land as they were able to cultivate, and beautiful forests. By 1699, the town had gained a glowing reputation among the French as being one of the best harbours on Nova Scotia's coastline.

More settlers arrived; the majority began fishing, farming, trading furs, and selling lumber, while others started shipbuilding and mast-making enterprises — activities that helped sustain the economy during the long and difficult winters.

After felling trees and working the land, the settlers coaxed cereals, peas, corn, cabbage, beets, onions, carrots, and turnips out of the excellent but rocky soil. Apple, pear, and cherry trees were transplanted from Normandy, creating a sense of home for the French-speaking settlers. The fruit and vegetable harvests, along with game the farmers hunted, helped create a self-sufficient community, which was critical since the city was isolated during the winter. When weather permitted, residents added a few frills to their supplies by trading raw materials and furs with New England sailors who brought cloth, rum, and farm and household tools in exchange. (After the Revolution, trading with the Americans was technically illegal, but settlers in coastal communities routinely broke the difficult-to-enforce law. The demand for supplies was simply too great.)

The industrious farmers not only cleared land and planted gardens, they also raised geese, hens, cattle, sheep, pigs, and goats. Grain, essential for bread and cake making, was sent to be ground at a mill in a nearby town. Almost every house had a spinning wheel, which women used to weave sheep's wool, hemp, and flax into clothing. The hardworking settlers began to reap the rewards of their enterprise.

Now and then the peace of the community was disturbed by pirates and looters who arrived by ship to harass and steal from the vulnerable settlers. The pirates were master mariners and anchored their boats down the coast, away from the vigilant eyes of the residents. They broke into houses and took whatever supplies they wanted. On other occasions, they operated on the water, taking over other boats, dumping the crew overboard, and grabbing any available goods.

Larger problems than pirates loomed on the horizon for the citizens of the small settlement. The 1713 Treaty of Utrecht that made Nova Scotia a British colony brought an end to French rule. It was to have grave implications for the future — even though it took more than four decades to unfold. During the intervening 40 years, life was deceptively peaceful. While some French settlers left the area voluntarily, others stayed on.

In 1755, Governor Lawrence of Halifax declared he was unwilling to accept the French settlers' resistance to pledging allegiance to the English monarch. He ordered that the Acadian French be deported to the American colonies. Less than a year later, the French settlers in Nova Scotia were forcibly removed from their homes, which were then raided and burned. The captives were sent to Halifax, and from there were shipped off to Europe. Families were split up and lovers separated in this dark and brutal incident in Canadian history — an ironic exchange when, just a few years later, the Loyalists who were banished in much the same fashion from the American colonies found refuge in Nova Scotia.

Once the area was cleared of French inhabitants, Governor Lawrence issued a proclamation "for the immediate settlement of this Province." He was anxious to populate the British colony with people loyal to the monarchy since those who were granted land would eventually pay taxes and fatten government coffers. Unless Canada was populated with Loyalists, the threat of being overtaken by the American States was a very real possibility.

Shelburne was considered an ideal location for English settlers, since English-speaking fishermen from New England had been using the shores for years as a base for summer fishing. Settlers were slow to come, though; wary and reluctant to leave their established homes. Spurred into taking more aggressive action, Lawrence issued another proclamation guaranteeing religious freedom for the immigrants. People suffering religious persecution in their own countries were attracted by the promise of freedom of religion though the proclamation had a fairly narrow scope, specifically excluding Roman Catholics and Jews.

Alexander McNutt, a native of Ireland living in the American colonies, organized a drive in the 1760s to bring new settlers to Nova Scotia. McNutt let it be known that settlers were to be granted land with the stipulation that the grantee clear at least one of every 20 plantable hectares within three years. On land unfit for cultivation, a good dwelling house had to be erected, otherwise the land would be confiscated and revert to the government.

The Loyalists Arrive

Shortly after McNutt's recruitment drive, a group of Scots-Irish settlers relocated to Nova Scotia while others straggled in from New England. Even so, the town's population remained sparse until the influx of Loyalists swelled the ranks. The first flood of refugees in May 1783 came as an enormous shock to the community of Port Roseway since the arrival placed an overwhelming demand on land and precious food rations. The small town was required to expand to find town lots for the new inhabitants. Six long streets ran north and south, and surveyors divided up parcels of land which were then drawn for by the Loyalists. The governor of Halifax, Governor Parr, came to oversee the land grants and set aside 200 hectares for himself.

On July 20, 1783, Governor Parr formally named Port Roseway after Lord Shelburne, the Prime Minister of Great Britain, and a great celebration was then held which lasted until five the next morning. In a letter to Sir Guy Carleton dated July 25, Parr said "From every appearance I have not a doubt but that it will in a short time become the most flourishing Town for Trade of any in this part of the world, and the country will for agriculture."

Having risked their lives for their British allegiance, some Loyalists felt entitled to the best parcels of land, creating tension between the newcomers and the residents. Although the residents themselves were far from homogenous. They were comprised of Dutch, Quakers, Germans, Blacks, Irish, and even a few French — and there was often conflict among them. Creating even more chaos were those feigning Loyalist sympathies to take advantage of the opportunities in a new land. Mutual distrust reigned.

The integration of the Loyalist refugees did not go smoothly in Shelburne. A shortage of surveyors in the town had a serious effect on the allocation of land grants. Many Loyalists waited a long time to receive their land. Black Loyalists waited even longer. The hastily constructed land-grant system broke down under the pressure of so many claims and corruption was commonplace. Land

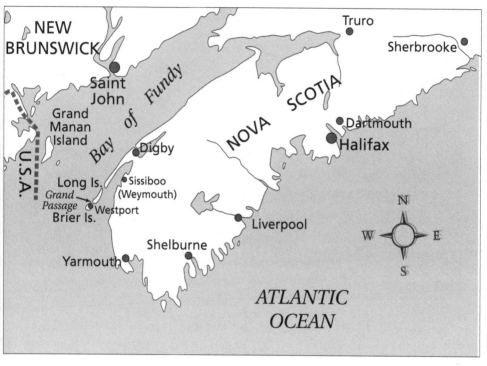

More than 35,000 Loyalists settled in the Maritime Provinces,
many in Nova Scotia, Canada's second smallest province.

measurement was done fairly casually and often incorrectly,
setting up generations of feuds between neighbours.

Settlements all across Nova Scotia felt the effects of providing accommodation for the influx of refugees and new
settlers. In total, 35,000 Loyalists ended up settling in the
Maritime Provinces, mainly in the port cities of Shelburne,

Shelburne Harbour from the town of Shelburne,
a watercolour by J.E. Woolford, 1817

Saint John, and Halifax. While the sheer numbers were difficult to deal with, another problem was the attitude of many
Loyalists who were used to a living a luxurious life and were
not equipped to face the hardships of making a new home for
themselves. Often the men lacked expertise in farming or
fishing. There was little sympathy from the British. A touring
officer stated, "Any man that will work is sure in a few years to
have a comfortable farm; the first 18 months is the only hard
time and that in most places is avoided, particularly near the

rivers, for in every one of them a man will catch enough in a day to last him a year. In the winter, with very little trouble, he supplies himself with meat by killing a moose-deer, and in summer with pigeons of which the woods are full. These he must subsist on until he has cleared enough to raise a little grain."

The British were determined to do well by the Loyalists, but housing and feeding the flood of newcomers was a haphazard affair well beyond their ability to control. Bureaucratic measures designed to help often became an impediment and as a result were ignored. Nova Scotia Governor John Parr's enthusiasm for the burgeoning community began to wane when reality set in. He showed his concern about the relentless tide of immigrants by going on record saying, "I have not yet been able to find any sort of place for them and the cold is setting in severe." Perhaps this is when the famous Maritime sense of community became established as refugees and members of existing towns rose above the tensions and politics of the time and reached out to help each other. Even so, many refugees, weakened from war and the arduous journey to Canada, died penniless from starvation and exposure during their first winter. Hundreds were buried without fanfare — graves dug in the frozen earth with an axe — and, since many of them were illiterate, their stories were never recorded.

Building a Home

Though the majority of Loyalists were tradesmen, farmers, merchants, fishermen, teachers, and clergy, every able-bodied man turned his talents towards building a home for themselves and their family. Each Loyalist family was given an axe, hammer and nails, saw and spade, a gun to share with five other families, and a whipsaw to cut house planks. The two sounds heard constantly in Shelburne's early days were the striking of an axe and the pounding of a hammer. There was a sense of urgency to complete the homes before winter arrived. The able-bodied men of the town also turned their talents towards building a town hall and fire hall for the fire engine that King George III had bequeathed the town as a token of his gratitude to his loyal soldiers.

Adam Hubbard and Eathel Davis took part in the construction boom, sometimes for pay and sometimes as part of a "frolic" — when neighbours arrived equipped with horses or oxen and helped construct a new building or clear land in exchange for a hot meal and a little socializing. Frolics were welcome diversions, although all too frequently the socializing turned into a drunken brawl.

By late 1783, Shelburne was transformed by the 1127 houses that had recently been built. By the end of 1784, another 300 dwellings had been erected. While the hastily constructed houses provided some shelter from the bitter cold, they were necessarily crude. They were built of logs with the spaces in between filled with a mixture of mud and moss.

The rudimentary plaster, made from a daub of pounded clamshells and sand, was then mixed with water to form a paste and used to cover the walls. The original settlers passed on skills they learned from the Native peoples, such as covering roofs with broad sheets of birch bark to keep out the rain — the same versatile material often used as paper for letters or land deeds.

A few of the more sophisticated houses built for the gentry had planks for roofs, covered with handmade shingles. Fancy or plain, none of those early homes had electricity or indoor plumbing. Generally, the houses were low, with a door in the centre and a window on either side. A massive fireplace built from handmade clay bricks provided heat and was used for cooking. In most cases, there was a single floor for living, eating, and sleeping, though many houses also had an upstairs loft.

As the Loyalists became established, they constructed furnishings for their houses by building birch and pine tables, chairs, and bedsteads, as well as household items such as jugs, cups and saucers, teapots, and spinning wheels. The women made butter and cheese, candles, soap and starch, and their own yeast. They brewed home remedies from the herbs they gathered in the fields and woods, along the shores, and in their gardens, and boiled spruce boughs for a liquor to which they added molasses for spruce beer. They spun both flax and wool, and wove linen and woollen cloth that they fashioned into clothes for their families. Once the Loyalists had provided basic lodging for themselves, they turned their attention to fishing and farming as their main sources of income, supplemented with the sale of lumber and animal skins.

A Different Form of Slavery

As this industrious group of people made Shelburne their home and settled in, an underclass was being displaced. Among the Loyalists seeking shelter in Canada were several thousand African Americans who had hoped to escape slavery by joining the British army. Black Loyalists had to wait up to six years for paltry land grants — a serious inequality that would simmer for generations to come.

Slaves had been perfect recruits for the British. Preoccupied with the war, owners had few resources to hunt down their errant slaves. By joining the army, African Americans were under the protection of the British, whose slogan "Freedom and a Farm" was seductive, though not entirely accurate. Of the tens of thousands of African Americans who declared themselves Loyalists, few of the 1500 who ended up in Nova Scotia became farmers.

When white Loyalists from the southern colonies later arrived with their slaves, many African Americans realized they'd simply traded one form of slavery for another. McGragh's Tavern doubled as a slave auction, and slavery was not officially abolished in Nova Scotia until 1833. Slave trading continued surreptitiously for a few years after.

Though the white Loyalists had just escaped a war, they weren't yet prepared to live peaceably with their neighbours. The majority resented David George, a black preacher, possibly because so many white Loyalists attended his church. One night, a vigilante crowd out for blood threatened the preacher in his church. "I stayed and preached," George said, "and the next day they came and beat me with sticks and drove me into a swamp." They also destroyed the preacher's house.

On July 26, 1784, the African American Loyalists were driven out of the town they had helped to build. "Great Riot today," deputy surveyor Benjamin Marston reported. "The disbanded soldiers have risen against the Free negroes to drive them out of Town, because they labour cheaper than they — the soldiers. (July 27) Riot continues. The soldiers force the Free negroes to quit the town — pulled down about 20 of their houses."

While many African Americans stayed and, against long odds, built a permanent community in Birchtown, David George threw in the towel and joined a second exodus of almost one-third of the black population, who sailed to Sierra Leone where they established the colony of Freetown.

It was into this world of high drama, conflict, great undertakings, and ultimately bitter disappointment that Margaret Davis and her family landed. But they didn't stay for long.

In fact, hundreds of people ended up leaving

Shelburne. The rocky terrain proved difficult for farming and many of the now-disillusioned Loyalists moved on to greener pastures. In their bitterness, they renamed Nova Scotia "Nova Scarcity." In 1792, the post office closed, and in 1802, Halifax postmaster Alex Cunningham reported "Only four letters for Shelburne," and later on, "Only one letter for poor Shelburne." By 1815, the population of Shelburne had been reduced to only 400.

By then, though, the Hubbards and Davises had long since left, looking for shelter elsewhere.

Chapter 3
Long Winter, Disastrous Spring

The decision of whether to move on to Quebec or stay in Shelburne rested on Adam and Eathel's shoulders, and both men felt the weight of that responsibility. Certainly they needed a house of their own, but since both families had finally been granted land in Shelburne, they felt it would be best to settle there, where they had the beginnings of a community, rather than venture into the unknown once again.

The ground was still frozen solid in March, so plans were made to begin construction on a home in late April. In the meantime, the two men, along with 19-year-old George Hubbard and 13-year-old Jacob Hubbard, found work wherever they could. Sometimes they helped build a new house, other times they hauled in fish. Between them, they managed to get enough food for the family.

Disaster Strikes

April 15, 1784, dawned damp and foggy. In was early morning when Adam and his son Jacob sat down to a large breakfast and several cups of coffee before heading out to check on a temporary lighthouse they had helped erect on McNutt's Island. Though only 13 and slight in build, Jacob was strong and happy to do a man's work. He much preferred working outside to being in school.

Because of the heavy fog that morning, rowing over to the island took Adam and Jacob twice as long as usual. A strong wind came up suddenly, and the waves grew steadily more menacing as they licked the top of the small rowboat. Finally, Adam and Jacob saw the island looming through the fog and pulled in as close as possible to shore. Scarcely able to see enough to put one foot in front of the other, Jacob got out of the boat and hurried ahead. But as Adam got out of the boat and pulled it to shore, he lost his footing and fell, striking his head on a rock. The next thundering wave took him out to sea, and each subsequent wave carried him farther out, beyond the reach of his frantic son, who was standing helplessly on the rocks. With his heavy woollen clothes and clumsy boots weighing him down, Adam didn't stand a chance against the capricious forces of nature. Still, he struggled against his fate as long as he could. Jacob resisted the temptation to go after him, knowing it was hopeless. Adam Hubbard was never seen again and his body was never recovered.

As he rowed home, Jacob grieved for the father he admired greatly and had worked with every day. His body shook as he pitted himself against the waves and wondered if he'd meet the same fate Adam had. He knew his father would want him to be brave and he was glad no one was there to see his tears mix with the salty seawater.

Imprinted on Jacob's memory for the rest of his life was his mother's face when she saw him walking up to the house alone.

"And your father, Jake?" she asked.

"Drowned Mam," he answered. "He fell, hit his head, and the waves took him just like that. There was nothing to be done for it. I tried."

Mother and son looked at each other a long hard moment and then Catherine embraced Jacob as they shared their grief. She had a small suspicion that she was pregnant and wasn't sure whether to rejoice or despair over the possibility. One more mouth to feed under these conditions was a daunting thought.

After Adam's death, Catherine, Eathel, and Margaret decided unanimously to decline the offer of land in Shelburne. The land they had been granted was not choice property and there was conflict and upheaval in the town — just the atmosphere they had hoped to escape by leaving the colonies. If they had to rebuild, they wanted to do so in an environment that would provide a tranquil life; a place where they could nurture their families, find work, attend church, and send the children to school.

Many other Loyalists had also become disillusioned with the state of affairs in Shelburne and had moved on. Some had slipped back inside the American colonies, hoping that the hard feelings had died down by this time. This was not an option that appealed to Catherine and the Davises, but neither was remaining in Shelburne. Catherine, more so than the others, felt strongly that a move would be best. She didn't want to live the rest of her life with sad reminders of her husband's premature death.

On the Move

Travelling with other disenchanted Loyalists, and still under the protection of the British militia, the two families left by boat for Sissiboo, Nova Scotia (later renamed Weymouth). Catherine later wrote: "We left Shelburne for Weymouth, Nova Scotia in July 1784 with a number of government vessels under the command of Captain Coonell; we, however, were in the charge of Captain Goldsburg of the British army."

On the voyage from Shelburne to Sissiboo, Catherine's feelings of nausea confirmed her suspicion that she was pregnant. While George and Jacob were now old enough to work and fend for themselves, she was still responsible for 16-year-old Ana Maria and 15-year-old Elizabeth. She worried about them, hoping they would find good husbands before long. But among the rough and ready immigrants in Nova Scotia, Catherine had seen few who would make good husband material. And those few were quickly snapped up by girls belonging to families with much better prospects than this poor widow was able to offer her daughters.

Finally, the weary group landed in Sissiboo, where they settled for the next four years.

Settling In Sissiboo

While life was more peaceful in Sissiboo, the families hadn't completely escaped conflict. The area's original immigrants were now settled enough to be resentful of the influx of new-comers. Food and supplies were scarce, and this alone created tension. With no police force to keep the peace, squabbles were regularly settled by locals who took the law into their own hands. From time to time, military officers arrived and did double duty as police officers, meting out rough justice on the spot. In most cases, a trial was out of the question.

Adding to the tension was the fact that the established settlers were mostly comprised of New Englanders who had been invited to come to Nova Scotia after the Acadian expulsion and before the American Revolution. Government officials openly questioned where the loyalties of these settlers really lay. They worried that if the American colonies decided to invade Canada, these transplanted pre-Loyalist New Englanders might well side with their former compatriots —

not so much because they believed in the larger cause, but more because they resented sharing their land and supplies with all the Loyalists newcomers. That Britain might then lose Canada to the Yankee cause was unthinkable.

After much discussion in the garrisons in Halifax harbour, it was decided that a separate province would be formed and called New Brunswick. New Brunswick would be settled with Loyalists who could be counted on to pledge allegiance to the Crown and take up arms if necessary. The province of New Brunswick acted as a buffer between Britain and Nova Scotia. The official proclamation from King George III, dated June 18, 1784, read "His majesty having taken the same into His Royal Consideration has thought it proper that the Province of Nova Scotia should be divided into two parts."

Catherine's Quest

In 1785, Catherine gave birth to her last child, Ruth Hubbard. Official birth registries weren't introduced until August 1864, so Ruth's exact birth date is not known. On August 14 of the same year, Margaret and Eathel Davis had their first child, Hannah Naomi Davis. Although Ruth was technically Hannah's aunt, the two girls grew up as sisters.

In Sissiboo, Catherine was faced with starting over yet again. She had no means of supporting herself and her family and was grateful to have Eathel to look out for her. But she was a feisty woman, prepared to do whatever it took to provide properly for her children. With her family's backing, she filed a claim for compensation for the land that was confiscated in New York. Since the period for making compensation claims had passed, her petition was initially rejected. So, leaving baby Ruth in Margaret's care, Catherine returned to New York to make her claim in court personally. The court rejected her claim a second time. Finally, armed with a declaration signed by the governor of New York dated May 12, 1786, this determined woman received a substantial sum of money from the State of New York.

Soon after Catherine received the compensation, she returned to Sissiboo. Now she had the funds to have Ruth baptized at the Anglican Church in Digby. Celebrations were muted because of the death of Adam Hubbard just two years previously. He was sorely missed.

In 1787, Eathel and Margaret had a second daughter, Sarah. Sarah was baptized in Digby on November 22, 1787. Soon after Sarah's birth, the families prepared for another move. With the money she'd been awarded, Catherine bought land on nearby Brier Island. She'd heard wonderful things about this isolated island and believed that, with a move to a tranquil, barely populated island, she would find the peace and quiet that had so far eluded her. All she wanted at this point was to raise her youngest child, see her girls happily married, and her boys gainfully employed.

Meanwhile Eathel had been granted land in Sissiboo and the two families contemplated building a permanent home there. Eathel had built a small cottage, but it was never intended to be a permanent home. Weary of constant confrontations between neighbours who were angry at the arrival of the newcomers, the two families pulled up stakes and moved to Brier Island.

Chapter 4
Brier Island:
Home At Last!

I t was 1789 when Catherine, Margaret, Eathel, and their collective children sailed the 30 kilometres from Weymouth to Brier Island and became the seventh family to settle there. Margaret Davis didn't know it at the time, but when she set foot on the island, she had found her true home — the place where she would spend the rest of her life. In the end, she helped shape the island as much as it shaped her.

The newcomers quickly learned the history of this enchanting but primitive island from the other residents. They were told that the first European settlers on Brier Island had arrived by serendipitous means 30 years earlier. In 1759, David Welch and a group of other fishermen were literally blown onto the island by a strong wind. Well, better the island than the treacherous rocks where others before them had perished! Welch and his men discovered a fisherman's paradise and filled their boat with fish before returning to Maine. The following year, Welch returned with his wife and built a cabin on Brier Island.

Over the next few years, a few other families, attracted by a thriving, albeit small, shipbuilding industry and the bountiful fish, settled on the island. With help from other locals, Elisha Payson built the first shipping vessel on Brier Island in 1783, six years before the Davis family arrived. Government subsidies for new ships built in the region gave further incentive to an already lucrative industry and attracted more immigrants to coastal towns with a fledgling shipbuilding industry. As long as ships were made of wood and driven by wind and sail, Brier Island thrived. (The island population continued to grow and by 1818, there were 147 inhabitants.)

In years to come, when ships began to be made of steel and were fuelled by steam, the population and industry base of Brier Island declined. But it was thriving when the Hubbards and Davises arrived, and they would soon become central figures in the growth, history, and development of Brier Island. Eathel Davis knew that he and his brothers-in-law, George and Jacob, could earn a decent living and provide for their families by fishing and shipbuilding there.

After hearing about the violent electrical storms that

frequently hit the island, the two families decided to build their new home alongside the other Loyalists in the town of Westport — on the sheltered inner curve of the island. The house would be large enough to hold all of them — at least for a while.

Canada Takes Shape

Shortly after Margaret and her family moved to Brier Island, the Constitutional Act of 1791 was passed, creating Upper and Lower Canada. The country of Canada, though not formally declared a nation until 1867, was slowly taking shape. Since the idea of paying taxes without representation had provoked the American Revolution, the British wanted to do things differently in Canada. The plan was for the Upper and Lower Canadian governments to be financed by reserving one-seventh of all the land for the Crown. Another seventh was set aside to finance the Protestant clergy. Since Canada had plenty of unpopulated land, this didn't cause resentment.

Wanting to influence the policies of the new country, the Loyalists who had led a privileged life in America petitioned the new government to retain the same system of titled aristocracy that England had. Their proposals were rejected, and so Canada ended up with a much less rigid class system than that in Britain.

In any case, maintaining status was tricky in a country where virtually everyone was starting life all over again and building from scratch. No matter how grand the ancestors, how deep the pockets, or how devoted the servants, each person's survival depended on hard manual labour — it was a great equalizer.

The arrival of Loyalists brought greater trade prospects for Brier Island. After America declared its independence from Britain, the British West Indies boycotted trade with the newly formed United States. The entrepreneurial Loyalists hastened to fill the gap in the marketplace. Americans had to stand by helplessly and watch precious rum, molasses, sugar, and salt sail past them to the Maritime Provinces where these goods were traded for fish, fur, and lumber. Nova Scotia became the foremost supplier of smoked herring, mackerel, salt cod, and wood to the Caribbean.

Starting Over

The Hubbards and Davises lived in cramped quarters in a boat where at least they were somewhat sheltered from the weather while Eathel, George, and Jacob cut down trees, dug out the stumps with crude tools and an ox, and built a cabin large enough for the extended family. With help from willing neighbours, the house was ready before long.

It consisted of one large room that served as kitchen, parlour, hall, and bedroom for the adults, while the children slept in an upstairs loft. While in other parts of the Maritimes, European immigrants turned up their noses at the common practice of placing the beds in the open space of the large room rather than hidden away under a handmade canopy, life on Brier Island was not as genteel. Since fishermen took their lives in their hands on a daily basis, appearances didn't account for a whole lot. As long as survival was paramount, practicality reigned. And while Margaret sometimes longed for a little of the luxury she had enjoyed back in New York, she was a practical woman and made do with what was available.

In the Davis residence, as in many others, a smaller, windowless room was built just off the larger room. Insulated with tree bark, it was used to keep dairy products and root vegetables cool. Pine shingles covered the log roof of the house. A large, pine china cabinet near the fireplace stored dishes, kettles, and candlesticks. Pine, particularly white pine, was the chosen wood of the Loyalists when it came to creating fine furniture.

When the garden produced its first crop, heads of Indian corn were hung from the beams inside the house, along with herbs such as savory, catnip, marigold leaves, and balm of Gilead buds tied in bunches. Dulse was left to dry in the shed. These assorted herbs were used for medicinal and culinary purposes.

Once the log cabin was built, Eathel's next priority was to build a frame barn. According to Frances Beavan, who wrote about New Brunswick in the 1800s in *Life in the Backwoods of New Brunswick*, "A frame barn is the first ambition of the settler's heart; without one much loss and inconvenience is felt. Hay and grain are not stacked out as in other countries, but are all placed within the shelter of the barn; these containing, as they often do, the whole hay crop, besides the grain and accommodation for the cattle, must, of course, be of large dimensions and are consequently expensive."

It was a great cause for celebration when the house, basic furniture, and the barn were finally ready. Neighbours joined in the frolic — women brought gifts of baked goods and the men arrived with rum to toast the new arrivals to the Island.

Daily Life

On a typical day on Brier Island, Margaret got up at 4:00 a.m. The noise of hungry animals wanting to be fed served as her alarm clock in the mornings. She gathered wood and put logs on the fire, fed the animals and collected the eggs, then hauled enough water from the well for the day's activities. Catherine attended to the babies while Margaret prepared a hearty breakfast, including eggs, bacon, porridge, fresh-baked bread, and churned butter. In the summer months, the breakfast menu would include a dish called codfish and "taters" (potatoes). Eathel milked the cows before he ate breakfast and then left the cabin for the shipbuilding docks.

While Catherine tended to the fire and looked after the children, Margaret spun wool or made clothes for her growing brood. Before long, she left her sewing to begin preparing the large midday meal. Author Frances Beavan describes a typical midday meal as follows:

A watercolour painting by Robert Petley, c. 1835,
showing a group of Loyalists on the move.

"The present meal consists of fine trout from the
adjoining stream, potatoes white as snowballs and ... some
fried ham and young French beans ... We have also a bowl of
salad and home-made vinegar prepared from maple sap, a
large hot cake made with Indian meal and milk and dried

blueberries, an excellent substitute for currants. Biscuits, of snow-white Tennessee flour, raised with cream and sal-a-ratus. This last article, which is used in place of yeast, or eggs, in compounding light cakes, can also be made at home from lye of the wood ashes, but it is mostly bought in town … A raspberry pie and a splendid dish of strawberries and cream with tea (the inseparable beverage of every meal in New Brunswick) forms our repast and such would it be in 99 houses out of 100 of the class I am describing."

The hearty midday meal was cooked over the fireplace oven, which roasted the face and hands and required extreme caution so as not to set one's clothes on fire. In those days, cooking accidents caused one-quarter of women's deaths. Though stoves were in limited use in the United States at this time, they hadn't yet made their way to Brier Island.

Close by the hearth was a wooden saltbox, which was kept near the fireplace to keep the salt dry, but also to use for smothering any escaping sparks, which remained a real and present danger. Eathel was in charge of providing the household salt, which he did by evaporating ocean water in a pan. The salt was also used for drying and preserving fish and meat.

Meals needed to be substantial by today's standards since every capable person was involved in physical labour virtually from dawn to dusk. No one knew what a calorie was, much less counted them. On Brier Island, a summer meal often included the edible mushrooms and many berries — teaberry, pigeonberry, blackberry, blueberry, and cranberry — that grew on the island. Eating utensils were a communal knife — the same one used to clean fish and cut rope — and carved wooden spoons. (Sailors simply used seashells as spoons.)

On a clear day, when the sun hit a certain mark on the floor, Margaret knew when it was 12 noon — time to call her husband in from the docks for lunch. Picking up a conch with a hole drilled in it, Margaret stood at her front door and blew sharply three times. It was the Davis signal, used over the years to call men from work, bring the children in from play, or call for a neighbour's assistance in emergencies or childbirth.

After lunch, the children returned to school. Brier Island's first school was built soon after the Davises arrived. Initially, the notion of formal learning had been a hard sell to many Brier Island residents, who saw no need for it. The economy, after all, depended on the physical labour of farming, fishing, and shipbuilding — not "book-learning." Eventually, with much grumbling, all those with children chipped in both funds and labour towards building supplies and the teacher's wages. It was common practice for people to band together to pay for the schoolteacher, who was expected to teach several grades at the same time. A local family provided room and board. The Nova Scotian government provided 20 pounds a year towards the schoolteacher's salary and the upkeep of the school. All six of the surviving Davis children attended the original Brier Island school, which stood until 1976 when it was washed away in a wild storm.

When the Davis children came home from school on chilly afternoons, the glowing fire welcomed them. And for Eathel Davis, who was by then weary of clearing land by hand, the blaze was welcome indeed since every log burned on the fire was one less on the land.

In the afternoon, Margaret soaked wool, which had been carded in a mill on the mainland, in water coloured brown by butternut bark or green using sweet fern and indigo. The dyed wool would later be knit or woven into clothes, hats, mittens, and blankets. As the babies slept, Catherine combined some of the animal fat left over from the noon meal with wood ash to make batches of soap. While that was setting, she poured cream into a barrel and beat it with a wooden ladle until it turned into a rich butter. The older girls took long pieces of string and dipped them over and over into melted wax, making enough candles for the week ahead.

At suppertime, the family gathered again for a meal, this time consisting of a hearty soup and bread, with pie or custard for dessert. The women cleaned up the dishes, the children did their homework, and Eathel put the finishing touches on another piece of furniture. Just before bedtime, a small verse from the Bible was read and, after prayers and a final trip to the outhouse, the children were sent to brush their teeth — with a toothbrush made of a stick with a piece of cotton wrapped around it and salt as a cleaner — then off to bed.

The industriousness of people living in the 1700s is almost beyond our imagination today. Work was sharply defined by gender, and it was considered against a woman's nature to work in the fields. While women's work was different from men's, they certainly worked as hard, if not harder. As a diligent mother, Catherine Hubbard had taught her daughter that to survive, she had to be resourceful. Passed on from mother to daughter to granddaughter were the techniques for needlework, lace making, knitting, soap making, candle making, spinning, and weaving, as well as healing skills for the inevitable childhood illnesses that came along.

The oldest Davis children, Hannah and Sarah, thrived on the fresh island air, but the first two children born on Brier Island — Alice, born in November 1789, and Adam, born in 1791 — died in infancy. Margaret grieved both deaths, but was especially heartbroken over the loss of her son, who had been named after her father. Eathel and Margaret had five more children; Margaret was born in 1792, Jacob in 1794, Amelia in 1797, Ethel Jr. in 1799, and Hubbard in 1801.

As her family grew, Margaret became more determined than ever to learn how to heal and to understand how to treat sickness. She persuaded her husband that tending an herb garden could be considered women's work, and she began learning about and nurturing plants that were known for their healing qualities. She learned much from her mother about traditional German ways of healing and also learned such Native medicinal practices as drinking a tonic comprised of spruce needles and water to ward off scurvy in the winter months. Soon Margaret was consulted by neighbours for her medical knowledge and she began assisting other families during childbirth or family emergencies.

In 1794, Eathel Davis purchased Lot 4 from Catherine Hubbard for 30 pounds. He wanted to build a larger house for his growing family. That year, there was a flurry of sales following the introduction of a provincial tax of 50 cents per head or $2 for landowners from all males over the age of 21. By this time, Brier Island's population had expanded with the arrival of more Loyalists who had been promised grants of land as soon as the surveys were received in Halifax. Sorting out land claims became more of a headache with each passing year and competing claim. Part of the problem was the very casual system of land distribution. The most popular method was for the lots to be laid out and assigned numbers on a card. The numbered cards were placed in a container, and in the presence of three male witnesses, each person withdrew a card. That number turned out to be the drawer's "lot in life." Land was distributed quite literally in a lottery.

Religious Customs

For Margaret's family and the other Loyalists on Brier Island, attending church was a huge social event. The church was a great place to congregate and greet old friends, and for young men and women of marriageable age to consort with each other. It also provided the perfect occasion to show off a new dress from "The Boston States" (New England).

When preachers first arrived on the island in 1787 (two years before Catherine Hubbard and the Davises arrived), 52 people of all ages were waiting to be baptized. The weather was so unpredictable on the island for so many months of the year, that it was rare for a pastor to be available. Consequently, if he arrived in the winter months, people were baptized in the frigid waters, even breaking the ice when necessary.

Margaret and her family were originally Lutherans, but, like many other Loyalists, they attended the Anglican Church on special occasions and their children were baptized under Anglican auspices. The church, though, was on the decline partly because Anglican priests at the time tended to gravitate towards large towns and became wealthy by buying and selling real estate — a side vocation that did not sit well with many of the congregation who were struggling to keep body and soul together. Many disillusioned Anglicans were swept up by and converted to the Baptist faith.

Baptist services were first held on the island in 1799. The souls of Brier Island residents proved fertile ground for evangelical religious leaders of various denominations who started holding services there, beginning with Reverend Roger Viets, a missionary pastor with the Church of England who baptized the island's first settler, David Welch, along with 51 others. Reverend Enoch Towner, a Baptist minister, did not live on Brier Island but journeyed there regularly to hold Baptist services. The fire and brimstone preaching so popular in those days was a source of great entertainment, as well as fear — especially for the children.

The "Great Awakening" was an evangelical movement that had swept through New England in the 1740s, creating a fervor focused on personal conversions and the need for a "new birth." This awakening came in part from a need for stability and security in the midst of a war. The Baptist revival services held on Brier Island on a regular basis from 1799 on were strongly evangelical. Converts became very dedicated to their newly found religion and often travelled 30 kilometres to attend services. Reverend Towner praised them "for faithfulness and promptness in crossing St. Mary's Bay even on dangerous seas."

Others, though, staunchly resisted the call to be born again and continued in a life of debauchery. David Merrill, a Baptist preacher who visited the island from time to time, wrote a letter to his superior despairing over the state of the souls on Brier Island. Perhaps the incident he described happened after the arrival of a shipment of potent Trinidadian rum. In any case, the report painted a highly unflattering picture of island life at the time. It was published in an 1810 report of the Nova Scotia Association of Baptists:

"I will begin with Brier Island," wrote Merrill. "The place was notorious for irreligion perhaps as much so, in proportion to its magnitude, as was Sodom, on the morning of Lot's escape. Last autumn or winter, brother Peter Crandall visited the island and preached to as many of the shy islanders as he could collect within hearing of his voice.

"At a late hour the Assembly was dismissed. He retired but ere soft sleep had closed his eyes, a messenger requested he would visit a house distrest. Without gainsaying he arose and followed him. Whilst on his way, in the first house he passed, he discovered a light, it came into his mind just to call and see how they did. He found them in the agonies of dying unto sin, a household distrest for sins committed and salvation infinitely needed. He saw their anguish manifestly such, as all must feel or die forever and observing their exercises such as he judged not expedient to be interrupted, retired in silence. The next house, he found and left in a similar condition.

"Going a little further, he heard a person in the field, manifesting by his sighs and groans, bitterness of spirit. Mr. Crandall turned aside and in silent wonder beheld, and left the sin-sick man. He was soon at the house whence they had sent for him. Here he found a company sorely oppressed with their load of sin, burdened by it, and longing to be free. Here he broke silence and pointed dying sinners to a loving saviour. On this never-to-be-forgotten island, in 16 of the 18 families that reside on it, were 33 hopefully born from above."

Margaret was not among the new converts. She resisted joining the Baptist Church until 1839 even though the church established itself on the Island in 1799. Her son-in-law, Samuel Bancroft, was ordained as a pastor in 1828.

A Wedding

On October 21, 1796, Catherine's daughter and Margaret's younger sister, Elizabeth Hubbard, married William McKinney in the Anglican Church at Digby, eight years after the move to Brier Island. Holding a proper church wedding indicated superior social status, since many families settled for getting married by a third party, not necessarily a clergyman, and considered it legal.

Since 1753, a law in England had decreed that, for a marriage to be legal and binding, church banns had to be published and a licence obtained. But in the colonies, these laws were not always practical and were often ignored. Clergymen simply weren't always available, and even when they were, not every settler could afford to pay for a church wedding. Neither could all the enamoured couples wait for a visiting preacher — especially when the woman was pregnant. So the resourceful residents of sparsely populated communities adapted to their circumstances and developed a local method of publishing the banns, which involved a ceremony called stumping. The names of the parties to be married and the announcement of the event to take place were written on slips of paper, which were then stuck on the numerous tree stumps bordering the road, so that anyone passing by could read it.

Elizabeth's wedding was typical of church weddings at the time. It was a rowdy one, and an excuse for drinking. Elizabeth wore her best homemade woollen dress and a garland of flowers around her head. After the ceremony, one of the male guests toasted the bride by drinking ale from a wooden bowl, which he then passed round to the other guests. A party and a dance in the church hall followed the ceremony, and while the women and children went home early, the men folk stayed with the groom and got thoroughly drunk. When Elizabeth's spouse, William, finally joined his bride for their honeymoon in a nearby cottage, they were soon roused by a dreadful racket — guns firing, shouts and yells, and the beating of drums, along with the fierce barking of all the neighbourhood dogs. This rude tribute to the newlyweds was a custom handed down from the French and readily taken up by local inhabitants. The only way William could get rid of the group was to go to the door and offer them whiskey and a few coppers.

At weddings, it was customary for the bride to bring a dowry of sorts. Catherine's savvy land investments had proved fruitful and she was able to provide Elizabeth with a dowry consisting of a couple of cows and sheep, along with a barrel of molasses, a barrel of flour or pork, and tea. The entire family turned out for the wedding, all dressed in their Sunday best.

Margaret as Practitioner

After the wedding, life on Brier Island for the Davises quickly returned to normal, and the family settled into a steady routine. Although Catherine Hubbard and her youngest daughter, Ruth, eventually moved to Digby to live with Elizabeth and her new husband, this didn't cause a great disruption. Margaret's daughter Sarah, now 13 and out of school, took over many of her grandmother's duties around the house, helping out with the younger children.

Margaret nurtured the roses that bloomed in the family's front yard by fertilizing them with crushed seashells. She was pleased the crops were doing well without needing too much extra attention, since she had little time to tend them. She was increasingly in demand among local residents for her medical expertise. Margaret served as the island's unofficial doctor (referred to in those days as a "Granny woman") until a physician moved to Westport in 1838. Practising medicine in the 18th century was a haphazard business based on rudimentary science, common sense, and some intuition. By all accounts, Margaret Davis had a good mix of all three and was very much counted on for her knowledge of anatomy, which also made her an expert at setting bones.

Margaret was asked to attend at births and deaths on

the island and across Grand Passage on Long Island. Almost half the children born in the mid 1700s died in infancy and many of the women giving birth died as well. Some of those who survived childbirth later died from one of the common diseases of the time, such as scarlet fever (particularly in children), throat infections, smallpox (though inoculations, invented by Dr. Edward Jenner in 1796, were sometimes successfully used), diptheria, tuberculosis, and cholera. Since two of Margaret's young children had succumbed to disease, she was particularly pleased when she was able to bring an infant safely through a bout of illness.

Margaret was often summoned to attend to sick neighbours in the middle of the night. With a lantern in her hand, and sometimes accompanied by Hannah, Margaret travelled the breadth of the island on foot to reach the infirm. She carried mustard plasters, herbal teas, and poultices with her. In later years, a road was built across the island, making Margaret's nocturnal visits much easier, particularly in the winter. When there was great urgency, she would take the horse and buggy though she preferred travelling by foot.

She continued to learn everything she could as medical science progressed rapidly in the 18th century. Margaret heard talk of an influential medical book — written by Dr. Buchan of London, England, and published in 1784 — that stated that a "lack of cleanliness causes putrid and malignant fevers" and that "it is well-known that infectious diseases spread by tainted air." Finally, a connection between illness and sanitation was being made.

Dr. Buchan attributed some infant deaths to the common practice of mixing wine (believed to heat and inflame the blood) with a child's first solid food, and the practice of giving a child laudanum to help them sleep. Dr. Buchan also decried the practice of sending the child to a wet nurse to suckle. "Mothers should suckle their own children," he stated, "unless they are of a delicate constitution or subject to hysteric fits."

Margaret heeded Dr. Buchan's advice on childcare, as well as his warning to fumigate the bedding of the deceased in brimstone. He also warned not to wear the clothing of the deceased — a common practice in those days — and to wash one's hands before visiting other patients.

A woman ahead of her time, Margaret did not subscribe to the common belief that tobacco provided health benefits. She thought that the "tobacco resuscitator kit," developed in 1774 with instructions to "blow smoke up the bottom, nose or mouth of the body to revive the deceased," was nothing more than superstition. She also adamantly opposed bleeding, which was still occasionally used to treat illness.

On New Year's Eve, at the turn of the 18th century, Brier Island residents celebrated along with the rest of the world. Together with the apocalyptic tales that have long accompanied the end of centuries, were high hopes for the future as the world moved into "the modern age." Margaret, Eathel, Catherine, and the children celebrated together with their neighbours — with rifle shots and drum rolls. It was a noisy welcome to a new century full of hope for the future.

Chapter 5
Life's Twists and Turns

hile it wasn't quite as momentous an event as the first boat being launched from the shipyard, there was still great excitement on the Island the day that shipbuilder Elisha Payson's second boat was to take its maiden voyage. The boat and crew planned to leave that same week for the West Indies to purchase sugar, molasses, oranges, and rum to bring back to Brier Island. Fiddlers had travelled from Sissiboo to take part in the launching ceremony, and Payson's young daughter, Mary, was to crack a bottle of fine French champagne over the ship's bow.

The boat was decorated with flags and bunting, and the deck was spotlessly clean when people began arriving for the ceremony. Margaret wore a silk dress she'd brought with her when she left New York and, along with the children, joined Eathel in a rowboat as they rowed from their home to the boat. All the ex-officers and their wives were to be onboard the ship during the launching ceremony. There would be dancing and partying afterward. When everyone was onboard, the ceremony began with homage to King George III. One man played the drums and the others sang God Save the King.

The men on shore knocked away the boat's blocks with their axes and the boat floated into the water. Mary broke champagne over the bow and christened the boat. Two boats towed the ship out to an anchorage and dozens of smaller craft filled with curious sightseers rowed alongside. It was a joyous occasion, dampened neither by the bitter cold nor the strong wind that blew that day.

Eathel began to raise the Union Jack on the mast but halfway up it got stuck and remained at half-mast. It was, people said later, an omen of the worst kind. Eathel was uncharacteristically unsteady on his feet that day. Although he had climbed the mast hundreds of times before without incident, this time his foot slipped, he lost his grip, and fell several feet to the ship's deck. Alarmed crewmembers rushed to his aid. They could see the bone poking through the skin of his badly twisted and broken leg. Margaret had witnessed her husband's fall and was among the first at his side. "Bring him home," she commanded the crew. "Now!"

Once at home, it took all of Margaret's skills to clean the wound with water and vinegar and reset the broken bone. Over the next few days, Margaret lovingly administered her legendary tonics and herbal remedies to her husband and was dismayed to watch him grow progressively weaker. The wound became infected and the infection quickly spread. Margaret suspected Eathel had sustained internal injuries as well as a broken leg. He developed a high fever and a sore throat, which rendered him unable to eat.

As the infection continued to spread to his vital organs, Margaret feared her husband would soon go into a coma. She did everything she could to nurse him back to health — she sang to him, prayed with him, brought him custards and soups from the neighbours, and told him stories of what was happening in the world. But nothing worked. Finally, the family was forced to acknowledge that he would not recover from his injuries. On May 11, two days before his death, Eathel Davis, with a wobbly signature, signed the will that Margaret and her brother-in-law had prepared for him.

Margaret was completely distraught at the thought of losing the man she'd loved so faithfully for so long — it was almost unbearable for her to think that the dashing sergeant who had endured so much in his life and been such a caring husband and father would not be around to enjoy his grand-children and grow old with Margaret. It worried both of them that Margaret was four months pregnant and that Eathel would not live to see this child born. One comfort to him, though, was that he was able to leave his family fairly well provided for. They had a roof over their heads, some live-stock, and two boats.

Eathel's will stated that the livestock were to be left to the children, "all my stocke to be equally divided among them — one pair oxen, three cows, 21 sheep" and the boats and his estate were left to his wife. Eathel died on May 13, 1801, at the age of 45. He left Margaret, at the age of 37, with six children to raise — four daughters, Hannah, 16, Sarah, 14, Margaret, 9, Amelia, 4, and two sons, Jacob, 6, and Eathel, 2.

After her husband took his last breath, Margaret washed and prepared the body for burial. His boat-building col-leagues made a simple coffin out of pine, which the women lined with black cotton. In the meantime, the body was placed on slabs of wood over chairs in the parlour for two days before the funeral. Women watched and visited during the day while men, sustained by rum, kept watch over the body at night. Neighbours dropped in frequently during the day and brought baked goods to ensure that no one who visited went home hungry. Catherine came from Digby with Elizabeth and her husband to attend the funeral, and stayed several weeks afterwards to help Margaret with the children.

The funeral was a simple ceremony, comprised of neighbours and kin. To provide entertainment, mourners sang folk songs — many from the "old country" — and told ghost stories. Eathel's shipmates spoke and then everyone gathered at the funeral raised their voice to sing the final verse of the hymn "At Evening Time":

> *At evening time there shall be light,*
> *Earth's day of storm is dying*
> *Sorrow and sadness take their flight,*
> *There shall be no more sighing.*

Margaret tossed a handful of dirt on the coffin before she left the gravesite. It comforted her that Eathel had been buried at the top of a hill and that the gravestone was visible from her parlour window.

Carrying On

Widows in the early 19th century faced few options. They had to endure the humiliation of being considered a burden on society and live either with one of their children or be taken in as a charitable case by a relative or neighbour. Margaret's case was a little different. Her medical expertise gave her status in the community. But while she was well respected for her knowledge, she wasn't well paid. Those who could afford to paid her in cash, but more often she was paid with an offering of a plucked chicken, some salt cod, or a bushel of potatoes.

On October 14, 1801, Margaret's last child, Hubbard Davis, was born. His grandmother helped welcome him into the world. Catherine also looked after her daughter until she regained her strength. Since she was still in deep mourning for her husband, it took Margaret longer than usual to get back on her feet. The family was worried by the deep sadness that enveloped her.

Eventually Margaret recovered from the labour, but there was an abiding sadness that never entirely left her. Her faith helped to sustain her through what she referred to as the "dark years." She kept herself busy with her very demanding household and community activities, but somehow her heart wasn't in it — a part of her had died with her husband.

Brier Island Becomes Modernized

Although Brier Island residents were isolated from mainland life, news travelled via the Digby newspaper and arrived with visitors who sailed into port. Fireside tales of piracy and plundering were told over and over again. One especially terrifying story involved a black-bearded Irishman, Edward Jordan, who, with his wife and a ship's mate, killed two crewmen and took over a ship he'd booked passage on, travelling from Quebec to Halifax. The captain of the ship, John Stairs, had escaped by grabbing a hatch cover and jumping overboard. He survived hours in the freezing water and was eventually picked up by a passing American ship.

Purely by fluke, a British warship discovered the pirated boat, *The Three Sisters*, in a Newfoundland cove and brought Jordan to Halifax for trial. His hanged, charred, and chained corpse hung near the foot of present-day Inglis Street, at the entrance to Halifax harbour, as a warning to other sailors. Margaret's sister, who lived in Halifax, wrote to Margaret about the unforgettable incident.

Slowly, as time went on, Brier Island became more connected to the world. In 1803, two years after Eathel's death, a lighthouse was finally constructed. That same year, a regular ferry service began carrying passengers to and from Brier Island. And later that year, a birth notice in the Digby paper noted that Samuel Edison was born in Digby, Nova Scotia. Years later, Samuel's son, Thomas, would invent the electric light bulb.

Mail delivery on Brier Island was uncertain at best, arriving at Digby and delivered by ferry once a week or so, and then hand-delivered to those who weren't able to pick it up. Lots of mail got lost on the way and hearts were broken when long-awaited love letters somehow went astray.

In 1810, mail delivery became more reliable when a local resident was given a government contract to deliver the mail on Brier Island. On mail day, chores were put off for a time while the precious letters from loved ones were read. The letters in German that Margaret received from her sister in Halifax and a few relatives who remained in the States were read, reread, and cherished.

In 1812, a road was built connecting Yarmouth and Digby, and a once-a-week mail service was established. Along with the mail came the newspapers from Halifax and Digby, which were shared among the settlers. On July 2, 1813, the *Halifax Weekly Chronicle* contained an advertisement for a new company, A. Cunard and Son, agents for vessels loading for London and West Indies. This was the beginning of the worldwide shipping company, Cunard Shipping Line.

And it was big news when, on February 14, 1816, the first Nova Scotia stagecoach left Halifax bound for Windsor. Six passengers paid $6 each to take the first trip. In high spirits leaving Halifax, they were a little bedraggled when they finally reached Windsor — 70 kilometres and 9 hours later. That might have been the highlight of the year for Canada's East Coast because the summer of that same year turned out to be a complete catastrophe.

Dark Summer of 1816

Fifteen years after Eathel's death, a momentous natural event had a devastating impact on the island. Three major volcanic eruptions that had occurred in distant places — St. Vincent Island in 1812, the Philippines in 1814, and an Indonesian island in 1815 — threw huge amounts of sulphuric acid and ash particles into the atmosphere. These particles blocked out sunlight and at the same time, allowed the earth's heat to escape. Although it was summer, a vast territory was cast into bitter cold and darkness. Canada was affected by the cold, as was the northeastern United States, England, France, and Germany. The result was an unprecedented series of cold spells with severe frost every night. Near the Great Lakes, on June 6, 1816, temperatures dropped from 30°C to 5°C within a few hours. It was reported that Quebec City, which was particularly hard-hit, received 30 centimetres of snow from June 6 to 10. An estimated 1800 people in Europe and North America died from the cold and the resulting famine.

A vivid description of the devastating effect of the weather was reported in a history of Madison County, New York:

"In 1816 came the 'cold season.' There was frost in every month. The crops were cut off and the meager harvest of grain was nowhere near sufficient for the needs of the people. The whole of the newly settled interior of New York was also suffering from the same cause.

"The inhabitants saw famine approaching. What little grain there was that could be purchased at all was held at remarkable prices and this scant supply soon failed. Jonathan Bently at one time paid two dollars for a bushel of corn, which when ground proved so poor that it was unfit for use: throwing it to his swine, they too refused the vile food. Every resource for sustenance was carefully husbanded; even forest berries and roots were preserved.

"The spring of 1817 developed the worst phases of want. In various sections of the county, families were brought to the very verge of starvation! One relates that he was obliged to dig up the potatoes he had planted, to furnish one meal a day to his famishing family."

Brier Island residents suffered enormously during this period — the high winds off the water added to their duress. A cloud of volcanic ash covered the land for the entire summer, making daylight scarcely visible. It seemed apocalyptic to residents — a dark night of the soul that resulted in a renewed religious revival, and an exodus to more temperate climates once the weather improved enough to travel. Residents had no idea this 'summer that never was' had been caused by volcanic eruptions, nor did they know that this weather change was an anomaly and not likely to occur again in their lifetime.

Margaret's sheared sheep died from exposure to the unseasonable cold, birds and other wildlife froze or starved to death, and crops rotted in the fields. Residents had counted on a good harvest to get them through the winter but food was so scarce that stories came from the mainland of people starving to death. Margaret reluctantly asked a neighbour to slaughter a couple of her cows to supplement her meagre rations. Not a single part of those cows was wasted.

Fighting for Survival

In 1805, Daniel Welch had petitioned the government for his share of his father's land declaring "On or aboute the year seventeen hundred and sixty three ... Joshua Welch settled upon Brier's Island, at the entrance of the Bay of Fundy, till then desolate and uninhabitted, and was particularly usefull at that place both in assisting many indigents persons who came to settle there and in affording relief and assistance to distressed and shipwrecked seamen who were frequently cast away upon that dangerous island."

Welch's petition was granted, throwing the land-grant system in great disarray since the Loyalist settlers had been granted most of the island's land. The two claims were in conflict.

As time went on, the tangled land claims issue on Brier Island became more troublesome. As a measure of the level of tension during this period, Margaret was forced to pay a fine for trespassing on her neighbour's land to get to her closest water supply. Margaret knew well that more trouble was brewing. A neighbour named Hatch claimed to own her land and insisted that she vacate her premises and give him the land he felt he was due. He showed Margaret the deed that Governor Parr had issued him with an 'x' marking the location of his land. Margaret couldn't read English but she could understand this — the 'x' was right on the land that she'd farmed for 39 years. Hatch insisted that Margaret show him her deed to the land, but she didn't have one. He then asked that she buy the land from him, but she refused. He threatened to file an official complaint and take the matter to the high court in Halifax. Local residents who tried to intervene and resolve the dispute had no luck.

Margaret's heart sank the day the official-looking envelope arrived from the Nova Scotian government, setting a court date and requesting her presence in court. If she failed to appear, the property she lived on would be awarded to her neighbour. By now, Margaret was in her 60s and her children were grown up. She wasn't concerned about herself but was determined to leave to her children the land and the house she and her husband had worked so hard to build.

After giving the matter a lot of thought, she knew what she had to do. The only option open to her was to travel to Halifax, even though she would have to travel on foot. It was a preposterous idea for a lone woman to attempt to walk 500 kilometres through thick forests dissected by raging rivers. But no alternative presented itself, so Margaret made preparations for the journey. She wanted to appear personally in court to legitimize her land claim. She was confident that, as a captain's widow and the daughter of a major in King George III's army, she would win the case.

Margaret's children were horrified and begged her not to undertake the trip on her own. They offered to accompany her but Margaret wouldn't hear of it. She was going and going alone. She persuaded her loved ones that they would only slow her down and that at their age, with their whole lives ahead of them, it made no sense to put their safety at risk. She, at the age of 64, had little to lose. She'd happily risk her life to save her land. Without her land, she said, she might as well be dead.

She asked the local shoemaker to add sturdy new leather soles and heels to her shoes, then packed a few clothing essentials for her court appearance, along with a jar of water and a loaf of bread. On March 28, 1828, at 4:00 a.m., neighbours rowed Margaret to Clementsport, Nova Scotia, where she spent the first night of her incredible journey with the Ditmars, German Loyalists who had also come from New York.

Before sending her off the next day, the Ditmars insisted she eat a good breakfast and kindly gave her a note in English that explained her purpose and asked for shelter. From Clementsport, Margaret began the 500-kilometre trek to Halifax, walking through Albany Cross, Dalhousie, New Ross, and Sherwood. The road between Halifax and Annapolis, first surveyed in 1774 and cleared in 1816, wasn't at that point suitable for wagon travel and was used mainly for mail delivery by horseback. It was a bumpy, windy road, often interrupted by streams and blocked by forests — it made for a very difficult journey.

Margaret met soldiers and farmers along the way who had settled by the roadside, and though they had little to share they opened their houses to her. The second night, after walking 24 kilometres, Margaret stayed with friends of the Ditmars who had been told to expect her arrival. Other nights, strangers who had heard tell of this modern-day Joan of Arc and were impressed with her courage took her in. Often her hosts gave her a note to take to a friend or relative of theirs a day's walk away and she would stay a night there. Word of her whereabouts came back to Brier Island at least in the first stage of her journey. But for several weeks there was no word at all and concern among her family and friends mounted as time passed. Margaret had no means of communicating with her family to let them know she was fine.

Although the walk was difficult and the weather unpredictable, Margaret found it was liberating to be away from the demands of everyday life. While there were days when food was scarce, she refilled her bottle of water at one of the streams and kept on walking. Hardship was something she was well used to.

When she came within view of the Annapolis Basin, she was confronted with a new difficulty. The large estuaries of the rivers meant she had to follow the water many kilometres inland before the river became narrow enough to cross. Sometimes she had to wait for the tide to go out and then navigate across the muddy river banks to the other side.

Finally she came to a small settlement called Mud Creek (now named Wolfville) and asked for help at the church there. The minister and his wife took her in and they made sure she was well rested and took a hearty lunch with her before she set off again the next day. The minister drove her as far as Windsor in his horse and buggy before he left her on the road and turned back. Her journey began again, but now she was nearing her destination and the roads improved remarkably.

Another two nights and she was on the outskirts of Halifax. She had written her sister before her departure and knew Christiana would be eagerly awaiting her arrival. On arriving in the city, it was almost nightfall. Margaret approached a stranger on horseback and asked him if he could direct her to her sister's home. As luck would have it, he'd served in the same regiment as Margaret's brother-in-law and offered her a ride. Margaret and her sister had a tearful reunion and then Margaret collapsed from exhaustion for a couple of days.

On the day of the court hearing, Christiana accompanied Margaret to see Sir James Kemp, the lieutenant-governor, at Halifax's Province House. (Known for being the finest public building in British North America, Province House was built with the labour of French and American prisoners who also laid the cobblestone streets Halifax is still famous for.) While Margaret both spoke and understood English, her verbal skills in German were much superior and it was fortunate that Sir Kemp spoke German. Margaret spoke eloquently about being granted land on Brier Island and told him of her journey to Halifax. Kemp found Margaret's claim to her land credible and her journey remarkable. He was impressed by the woman's fortitude and issued a grant for the lands she claimed dated May 3, 1828. When Hatch later arrived by boat in Halifax, cursing and swearing about being cheated out of his land, the lieutenant-governor sent him away.

Margaret spent several days resting in Halifax. The reunion with her sister was wonderful and Margaret found it very difficult to part with her when it was time to return home. They knew it was unlikely they'd ever see each other again.

The return journey was less traumatic for Margaret. At least she knew of houses that were open to her along the way and people who had insisted that she stop by on her way back home. She felt she had divine guidance every step of the way.

The journey to Halifax and back took eight weeks. The day Margaret returned by sailboat from Digby to Brier Island, she was scarcely recognized at first. Who was this bedraggled woman, no more than skin and bones, slowly climbing onto the wharf? It was Eathel Junior, now a young man of 29 working on a boat in the harbour, who first spotted his mother and rushed to help her home.

Word soon spread through the island and the family gathered round as she told the story of her incredible journey. She'd gotten lost several times, she told them, once for two days, but had refused to panic and had eventually found a road that led to a cottage where she'd stayed overnight. Many other people had put her up during her sojourn, and she had been treated with kindness every step of the way.

Margaret's return to Brier Island was cause for celebration. She was triumphant and had won her land claim. A good cup of tea, a hot, home-cooked meal, and a good night's sleep were all she needed to set herself right. She was rightfully proud of herself.

Epilogue

Margaret's life was peaceful at last. But, always an active woman, she was more in demand than ever for her medical skills. Margaret's expanding expertise gave her a reason for carrying on through her long years of widowhood. She was truly a medical pioneer — though never officially recognized as such. (It wasn't until 1849 that a woman received medical certification in North America.) As her skills developed, so did progress on Brier Island, and life became just a little easier as a stronger connection with the mainland was made.

One memorable event took place soon after Margaret's return from Halifax. Brier Island gained a formal ferry service, bringing visitors and residents back and forth to Long Island, where they took another ferry to access the mainland. This brought revolutionary change to the island. A resident wrote in the *Digby Courier*:

> *"Recent arrivals augmenting our population have also tended to enliven us. We note quite a number, formerly residents here, who dain this tight little isle their birthplace. Emerging from the sultry, exhaustive atmosphere of the American cities and towns, the transition in a few hours, via Yarmouth is most grateful to their senses, where a whiff of the old Bay of*

Epilogue

Fundy air, surcharged with the choice ozone, with a smack of humid fog sandwiched in by way of variety now and then, becomes a veritable life-inspiring tonic which one can take and not make a wry face."

In the same year that Margaret walked to Halifax, a group of leading Nova Scotian Baptists formed the Nova Scotia Baptist Educational Society and purchased a 25-hectare farm in Wolfville. On May 1, 1829, Horton Academy opened in a small, two-room farmhouse with 50 boys enrolled. Ten years later, Acadia University was built to accommodate the need for higher education for Baptist clergy. Acadia added a Ladies Seminary as well, to educate women. Four generations of Davises attended that institution.

Margaret Davis knew she had lived a remarkable life. Her sons and daughters had 44 children and 100 grandchildren between them. The matriarch had weathered much historical and personal drama. Her German reading and writing skills had grown a little rusty over the years and she couldn't read or write in English. So, surrounded by Hubbard Davis, her youngest son, his wife, and Margaret's grandchildren, Emiline, 23, Sarah, 20, Ben, 22, Jacob, 18, and Sam, 15, Margaret dictated her life story to her avid listeners. Her story was captured in *Glimpses of the Past From Long and Brier Islands.*

Margaret Davis died peacefully in her sleep two weeks later on February 11, 1858, at the age of 93. There was a full house for her funeral service, held at the local Baptist church. The remarkable woman had touched (and saved) many lives during her long life.

Christiana Margaret Hubbard was buried alongside her husband in the Baptist cemetery. The inscription on the headstone reads:

Hear what the voice from Heaven proclaims
For all the pious dead;
Sweet is the savor of their names
And soft their sleeping bed.

Appendix
Medicinal Plants
of Long and Brier Islands

People of the past looked to nature for many of their needs. They harvested the abundant forests to build their homes, and collected plants and hunted animals for food. Like other newcomers to North America, the early settlers of Nova Scotia discovered medicinal properties in the plants around them. Some were discovered by accident, others by trial and error, and still others were learned from their neighbours, the Mi'kmaq.

Paula Swift, a former resident of Brier Island who now teaches Grades 5 and 6 across Grand Passage at Freeport, Nova Scotia, has compiled the names of wild plants that were likely used by the Loyalists for medicinal purposes when first settling the islands. These are some of the plants Margaret Davis used for healing her patients.

Blue violet
Vitamins A and C are found in the leaves and flowers of the blue violet. Eating a half-cup of the leaves will give you as much Vitamin C as eating three oranges. Prepared properly, the flowers can be used to soothe an upset stomach and also make a great cough syrup.

Butter-and-eggs
When mixed with milk, this plant's juice makes a fly poison.

Clover
The whole plant is edible and can be eaten raw or cooked. The leaves and stalk are high in protein. The flowers can be made into a medicinal tea that is good for colds, coughs, and bronchial conditions. Let the flowers dry for about three days then pour boiling water over them and let them steep. The seeds and flowers have also been used to make bread in times of famine in the British Isles.

Coltsfoot
The leaves of this plant are used as a remedy for coughs and lung irritations. Cough drops can be made from the leaves by boiling one ounce of fresh coltsfoot leaves in one pint of water until there is a cupful of liquid left. Strain, add two cups of sugar, and boil until a drop of syrup forms a hard ball in cold water. Pour the syrup onto a buttered cookie sheet and allow to cool. Break up into small pieces before it becomes too hard.

Common St. John's wort
On St. John's Eve people would gather this plant to hang on their door and windows to ward off evil spirits and thunder. An ointment can be made from the flowers and it is also known to remedy melancholia.

Common wild rose
Rosehips have 25 times more Vitamin C than oranges. You get

Triadenum virginicum, a native St. John's-wort

as much Vitamin C from three small rosehips as you do from one large orange. The seeds also contain Vitamin E. Rosehips are an excellent emergency food and are available most of the year. A tea can be made from ground, dried rosehips or dried flowers. Add two tablespoons to a cup of boiling water and let steep. A little honey or sugar will bring out the fragrance.

Rosa sp., rosehips

Fireweed
Young leaves and stems can be eaten as greens and the older ones can be made into tea. The Native peoples used cooked roots as a cure for boils.

Indian-pipe
Native peoples used this white plant as an eye lotion.

Pitcher-plant
It has been suggested that Native peoples used this plant to make a potion used to fight smallpox.

Appendix

Spotted-touch-me-not
Spring roots can be eaten after boiling in water. The plant can be used as an antifungal and the juice from the stem can be used to soothe poison ivy rash and nettle stings.

Tansy
It was believed that this plant could be used to treat intestinal worms. It was also used to stimulate a person's appetite. Sprains and tired muscles were treated with a solution from boiling the leaves.

Wild strawberry
The leaves and berries of the wild strawberry are also high in Vitamin C and can be made into tea by adding a handful of leaves to two cups of boiling water.

Wintercress
Wintercress is eaten as a spring green. Its leaves have about three times as much Vitamin C as oranges. Early settlers used it as a cure for mild cases of scurvy. The young flower looks like broccoli and has even more Vitamin C than the greens. The flowers were boiled and served with salt and butter.

Yarrow
Yarrow can be made into an ointment or a milfoil tea to help remedy melancholy. The leaves can be chewed for relief from toothache.

These plants can be found in June Swift's *Brier Island's Wildflower Field Guide*. Information about the plants was taken from *Atlantic Wildflowers* (Griffin, Barrett, and MacKay) and *Edible Wild Plants of Nova Scotia* (MacLeod and MacDonald).

Bibliography

Beavan, Frances. *Life in the Backwoods of New Brunswick.* St. Stephen, N.B.: Print'n Press Publications Ltd., 1980.

Cuthbertson, Brian. *Wolfville and Grand Pre: Past and Present.* Halifax, N.S.: Formac Publishing Company Ltd., 1996.

Davis, Ralph Harold. *The Davis Family 1690-1997: A History and Genealogy.* Sentinel Printing, 1997.

Green Head. *Throw Out the Life-Line Across the Dark Wave: Westport Baptist Church, Brier Island, Nova Scotia.* Hymnal History from 1809, 1976.

McCormick, Roland K. *Faith, Freedom, and Decomcracy: The Baptists in Atlantic Canada.* Tantallon, N.S.: Four East Publications, 1993.

McInnis, Edgar. *Canada: A Political and Social History.* Toronto: Holt, Rinehart, and Winston, 1969.

Robertson, Marion. *King's Bounty: A History of Early*

Shelburne, Nova Scotia. Halifax, N.S.: Nova Scotia Museum, 1983.

Shea, Phil. *Brier Island: Land's End in the Bay of Fundy.* Windsor, N.S.: Lancelot Press, 1993.

Slocum, Joshua. *Sailing Alone Around the World.* New York: Penguin Classics, 1999.

Acknowledgments

Writing a book is always a communal effort and I am deeply grateful to all those who assisted me. Thanks to those whose help has been invaluable: Ralph and Cynthia Davis and Frank Davis for their painstaking research into the Davis family; John Clulee, president of R.H. Davis and Company, for sending me Ralph Harold Davis' book *The Davis Family of Connecticut, New York, Brier Island, and Yarmouth, Nova Scotia 1690-1997: A History and Genealogy*, on which much of this material was based. Direct quotes from *The Davis Family*, *The Backwoods of New Brunswick* and *King's Bounty: An Early History of Nova Scotia* have been used in this book.

Thank you to Paula Swift, teacher at Freeport, Nova Scotia, who supplied valuable material and read the manuscript. Also to Dorothy Outhouse of the Islands Historical Society, Brian Hicks of TIANS, Betty Stoddart of the Shelburne Museum, and Roland McCormick, author of *Faith, Freedom, and Democracy*, for so generously sharing their resources with me.

About the Author

Cathleen Fillmore has written three books and more than 200 articles. She is director of Speakers Gold (www.speakers-gold.com http://www.speakersgold.com), a Toronto-based speaker's bureau, and she coaches those getting into the field of professional speaking.

Photo Credits

Cover: National Archives of Canada, C-168 (ID#10192); History Collection, Nova Scotia Museum: page 38 (78.45.62); National Archives of Canada: page 27 C-17511 (ID#20680); National Archives of Canada / Robert Petley: page 59 C115424 (ID#20074); Natural History Collection, Nova Scotia Museum / Alex Wilson: page 96 (B01281) and page 94 (B00748).

THE HALIFAX EXPLOSION

Surviving the Blast that Shook a Nation

"Suddenly, a terrible blast jolted Andrew Cobb out of his reverie. It felt as though a giant hand had smacked the train, tipping it up at a precarious angle before dropping it back to the tracks with a crash."

A boat full of explosives heads in to the harbour as a large cargo ship steams out to sea. What happened next, on a fateful day in December 1917, is etched in history. At least 1900 people lost their lives and 9000 were injured when the largest man-made explosion ever experienced ripped through Halifax and nearby Dartmouth. Panic reigned as the survivors struggled to comprehend what had happened.

 True stories. Truly Canadian.

ISBN 1-55153-942-X

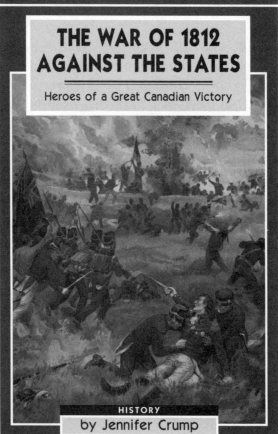

AMAZING STORIES™

THE WAR OF 1812 AGAINST THE STATES

Heroes of a Great Canadian Victory

HISTORY

by Jennifer Crump

THE WAR OF 1812 AGAINST THE STATES
Heroes of a Great Canadian Victory

"Issac Brock was a natural leader with a reputation for boldness and quick thinking. His ability to bluff was legendary... 'Most of the people have lost confidence. I, however, speak loud and look big.'"

In 1812 the United States invaded Canada. This exciting account of the stalwart defence of Canada and the ultimate victory over the American foes is told through the stories of six men and women involved in the conflict. The war united the young country and helped create a fierce new Canadian patriotism.

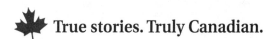 True stories. Truly Canadian.

ISBN 1-55153-948-9

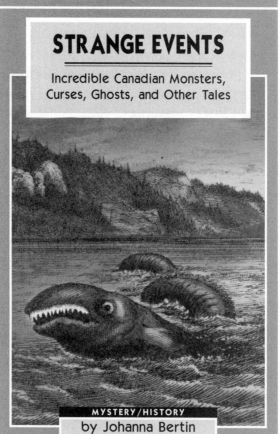

STRANGE EVENTS
Incredible Canadian Monsters, Curses, Ghosts, and Other Tales

"Nicholson was shocked when a 'dazzling light and shrieking whistle' came out of nowhere and headed right for his train. Paralysed with fear, he... swore that the passengers in the ghost train's lighted cars had looked directly at him."

What are the chances of being hit by lightening three times in one lifetime? And then, being hit again after you are dead and buried? This is just one of the incredible legends in this fascinating collection. From ghosts lurking on board mystery ships to the dark and chilling secrets of Niagara's devil's playground, Canada's history has never been so thrilling.

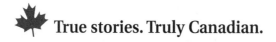 True stories. Truly Canadian.

ISBN 1-55153-952-7

OTHER AMAZING STORIES

These titles are available wherever you buy books. If you have trouble finding the book you want, call the Altitude order desk at 1-800-957-6888, e-mail your request to: orderdesk@altitudepublishing.com or visit our Web site at www.amazingstories.ca

New AMAZING STORIES titles are published every month. If you would like more information, e-mail your name and mailing address to: amazingstories@altitudepublishing.com.